I0759040

VAPOR QUEEN SAID SO!

Answers to commonly asked "how do I" questions when purchasing and setting up a hookah

Vapor Queen said so

answers to commonly asked "how do I" questions when purchasing and setting up a hookah

INTRODUCTION

Hey Hookahholic!! Thank you for purchasing my book! My name is Denise Michele. I was born and raised in Hempstead, Long Island, New York. I launched a brand called NY Vapor Queen. NY Vapor Queen was the first Mobile Hookah Bar to hit Long Island. At the time most people barely knew or understood what Hookah was. I would need to explain its use everywhere I went. Hookah has now developed into a huge industry. Many people are purchasing their own hookahs for personal use. For my anniversary as "Vapor Queen", I decided to create an easy step by step hand book that answers the most common questions I receive about purchasing and making hookah. Enjoy!!!

TABLE OF CONTENTS

Which Hookah Should I Purchase?

Full size table top hookahs and large floor size hookahs give you the best smoke.

Common mistakes:

Purchasing a miniature hookah- although they're cute they tend to malfunction easily. If you do get it to work properly it's still a mediocre smoke experience.

be sure to check the air release valve upon purchase. Unscrew it and make certain the metal ball is inside

SHAHIL MAAMOON

WHICH BOWL SHOULD I BUY?

I personally prefer to use a glazed clay bowl and I would recommend you do the same. The Shisha burns better in a clay bowl, which gives a smooth smoke experience

Common mistakes:

Using the bowl that comes with the Hookah you've purchased- they're usually very flimsy ceramic bowls and the tobacco burns fast which can lead to a harsh taste and cause coughing.

WHAT SHISHA SHOULD I BUY?

It's a matter of numerous preferences. It depends on what flavor, consistency etc.. that you like. Personally, I predominantly use Alfaker. I dibble and dabble with other brands.

Common mistakes:

Using Shisha that is too wet- if your shisha is very wet it won't burn properly. You would need to wrap it in a paper towel to remove some of the moisture so it doesn't leak while you're smoking.

Using Shisha that is too dry it's either old or wasn't covered properly after the last use. If it's dry, mix it in with moist shisha to give it life.

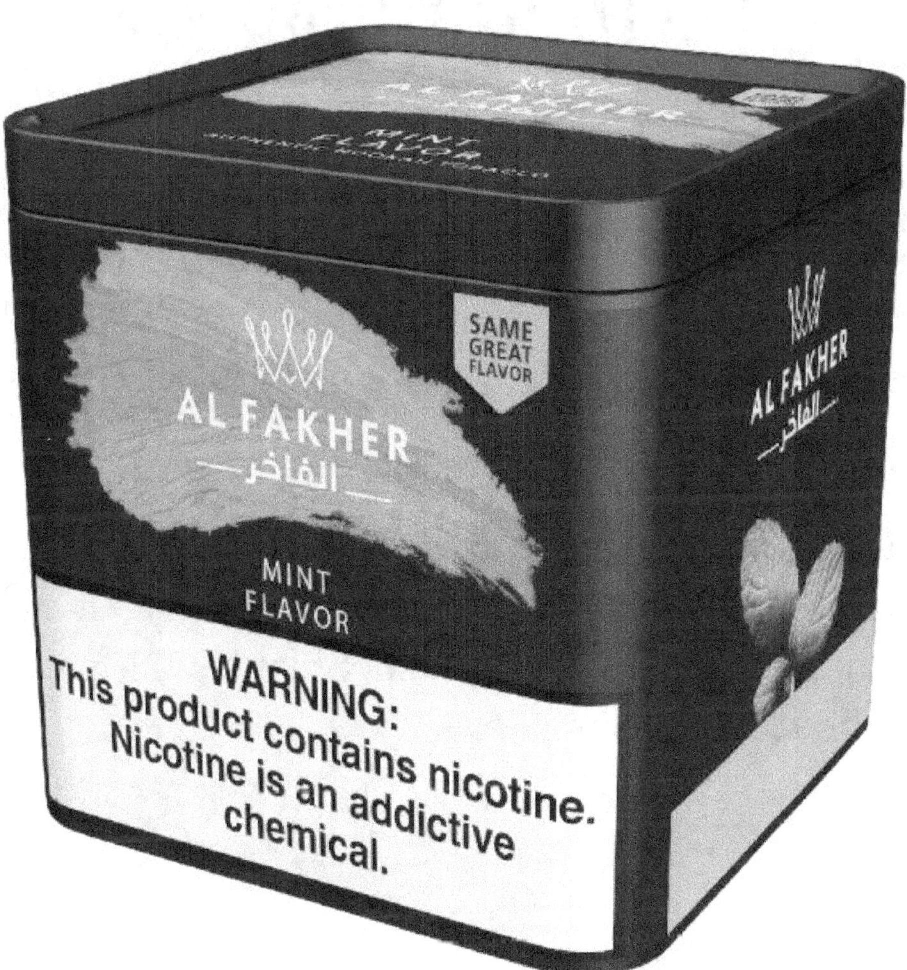

Smoking-Hookah

How much Shisha do I put in the bowl?

The Shisha should not exceed the brim of the hookah bowl. Pack it loose leaving room for the Shisha to breathe. Do not overpack your hookah bowl.

Common mistakes:

Overpacking the hookah bowl- Many people believe the more shisha they pack in the bowl the longer it will last. That is not the case. Too much Shisha will cause it to stick to the foil and burn

How do I poke the holes in the foil?

Foil holes should be pin size. I always suggest that beginners use a thumbtack to place the holes in their foil.

I am not a fan of already made Hookah foil but if you do decide to buy it make certain the foil is thick and it's large enough to cover the entire top of your bowl with holes (not just the center)

Common mistakes:

Making the holes too big- by doing this the Shisha will burn and the ashes from the Hookah Charcoal will fall through the foil holes and cause irritation to the throat.

Buying the wrong consistency and size of pre-punched foil- Yes it may save you a few minutes to buy foil that's already prepped but using regular foil and prepping it yourself is usually a better smoke.

Applying foil loosely- Your foil should be tight like a drum if it's loose your hookah will not burn properly.

HOW MUCH WATER DO I USE?

Your hookah stem should be submerged a half inch and no more than 1 inch.

Common mistakes:

Using too much water- when the water exceeds more than an inch of the stem, the water will more likely come through the hose when you smoke. This will also cause less smoke clouds.

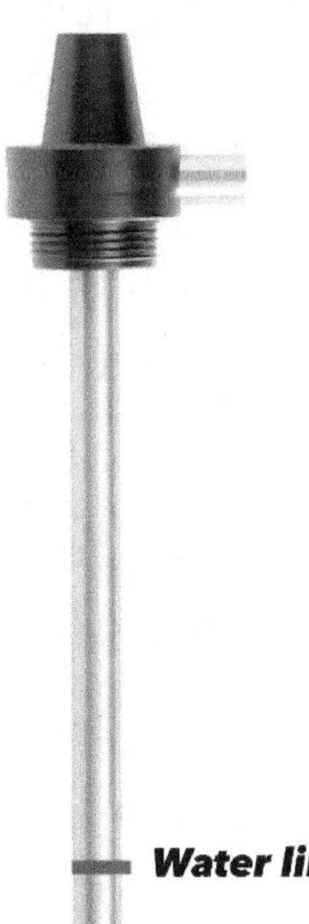

Water line

WHICH HOOKAH CHARCOAL SHOULD I GET?

It really is a matter of preference. I personally like to use coconut (coco Nara)square coals when I'm home. I'm not in a rush when I'm home and I can take my time to heat them on the stove. When I'm out traveling with my hookah I buy Starlight quick light large round coals. It's convenient and can be lit with any lighter.

Common mistakes:

Choosing the wrong brands and the wrong size-The hookah charcoal you choose can greatly affect the way your hookah burns.

Using too much or too little hookah coals- depending on what type of bowl you have and the size of your bowl will be the determining factor. If it's a smaller bowl 1 to 1 1/2 coals and if it's a larger bowl no more than three square coals or two round coals.

ECOLOGICAL
COCO
NARA
COCONUT SHELL CHARCOAL
فحم قشور جوز هند
120
PIECES
OF ART

100 pack
STARLIGHT
Superior Quality
Charcoal
Charbon de
qualité supérieur
100 40mm Instant Light Charcoal Tablets
100 Briquettes de charbon de 40mm à braise instantanee
Ignites Quickly - Allumage rapide
STARLIGHT

How do I clean my hookah

It is fine to just use soap and water. I also use a silicone bottle brush (it doesn't scratch the glass) and gadget to reach all the areas. If you have an all glass see through hookah I would suggest using rubbing alcohol and salt mixture to clean it and follow up with soap and water.

bottle brush set can be purchased on Amazon.com

Common mistakes

Not properly cleaning your hookah after use. A dirty hookah can lead to passing germs and becoming ill.

NY Vapor Queen began as a one woman show in March of 2015. It was just myself traveling as a mobile hookah service, renting out hookah to various venues. Shortly after I formed a team to cover more ground. I can proudly say that My brand has recently expanded beyond Hookah. NY Vapor Queen is an entertainment company that services all aspects of the nightlife industry. My journey is by no means easy as the brand continues to grow.

Thank you to everyone that has been supportive of myself and my brand, which goes hand and hand! I encourage every entrepreneur to stay focused on your vision and follow your intuition! Feel free to follow my progress on all the following media platforms

Xoxo

Denise Michele

I hope you found these tips helpful. If so, post the cover page in your IG or snap story and tag me with a thumbs up or tweet about it.

Thank you in advance

IG: @nyvaporqueen

Twitter @denisemichele19

Snap: Vapor queen

Clubhouse: Denise Michele

VAPOR
QUEEN

www.ingramcontent.com/pod-product-compliance
Lightning Source LLC
Chambersburg PA
CBHW081749280726
48658CB00023BB/2822